ENTERPRISING

THE VISION BOARD

NIKHIL MADUSKAR

Copyright © Nikhil Maduskar
All Rights Reserved.

This book has been published with all efforts taken to make the material error-free after the consent of the author. However, the author and the publisher do not assume and hereby disclaim any liability to any party for any loss, damage, or disruption caused by errors or omissions, whether such errors or omissions result from negligence, accident, or any other cause.

While every effort has been made to avoid any mistake or omission, this publication is being sold on the condition and understanding that neither the author nor the publishers or printers would be liable in any manner to any person by reason of any mistake or omission in this publication or for any action taken or omitted to be taken or advice rendered or accepted on the basis of this work. For any defect in printing or binding the publishers will be liable only to replace the defective copy by another copy of this work then available.

Contents

Preface

THE HUMAN EXCELLENCE NETWORK WAS CREATED AND ENVISIONED BY NIKHIL MADUSKAR AND HE HIMSELF HAD APPOINTED TWO CO-FOUNDERS IN ORDER TO TAKE THE VISION FORWARD BUT HAVE NO DIRECT CLAIM TO THE SOURCE OR THE VISION AS THIS VISION WAS INSPIRED BY SOMEONE WHO IS VERY DEAR TO THE AUTHOR AND THIS VISION WAS PENNED DOWN BY NIKHIL MADUSKAR THE AUTHOR OF THIS BOOK.

ANYBODY WHO WISHES TO TAKE THESE IDEAS FORWARD CAN GET IN TOUCH WITH THE AUTHOR BY MAILING AT MINDHACKNFSI@GMAIL.COM.

CHAPTER ONE

Legacy Studios

LEGACYSTUDIOS

A. THE CONCEPT -

1. Exclusive Personal Training- One on One and Group Training.

2. Certified Personal Trainers to train maximum 3 clients per slot.

3. Certification from ScienceBuilt in Personal Training and Nutrition.(Franchise Owner)

4. Business Concepts and Management from PWPL. (F.O)

5. Social Media Marketing Course and Grooming for Online Platform.(F.O)

6. Personal Transformation. (F.O)

7. Complete Gym Set Up .

8. Social Media Tools (DSLR, Laptop, Camera Accessories)

9. Quarterly Back-end Content and Knowledge Support for first year of establishment.

10. Marketing Package with Local Analysis.

B. THE CONCEPT- Services

1. Personalized Training Programs.

2. Specialized Group Sessions.

3. Nutrition Programs.

4. Online Training – One on One and Group.

5. Specialized Training Programs.

C. INVESTMENT

1. Gym Set Up – 1000k to 1500k.

2. Certifications – 50k.

3. Social Media Course and Grooming – 10k.

4. Social Media Tools – 100k.

5. Franchise Fee and Backend Support – 100k.

6. Marketing Package with Analysis – 50k.

TOTAL – 13,00,000/- to 18,00,000/-

Overheads Rent – 15k to 25k for 800qft to 1500sqft.

D. TARGET AUDIENCE

1. Metro and Tier 1/2 Cities.

2. For Set Up – Individual should be educated and fluent in English. (If need be, we will teach English)

3. Many from I.T sector shift to a career in fitness as it is more rewarding and freedom of work as it is self-employment and improves quality of life and not just standard of living.

4. Studio to cater upper middle class (those in I.T and MNCs) and the rich who can afford specialized training and attention.

E. REVENUE GENERATION

1. Personal Training Fees Ranging From 8k to 25k per month as per sessions.

2. Total Clientele 8 per trainer. (Per month revenue from P.T 64k to 200k)

3. Online Clientele 5 per trainer with package from 5k to 7k (REV – 25k to 35k)

4. Online Nutrition Programs @ 2500 per month clientele min 5 (REV – 12.5k min)

ESTIMATED TOTAL REVENUE PER MONTH – -101k to 250k.

ESTIMATED ANNUAL REVENUE – 12,00,000/- to 30,00,000/-

Note -

1. 90% of the investment required is made in machinery and education.

2. Knowledge and grooming are skills that remain for a life time and are essential for business.

3. Machine built quality being top notch, have a long life of 10+ years.

----xx----

ANSWERS TO YOUR QUESTIONS -

1) Think about monthly fixed and variable expenses

Fixed Expenses -

a. Rent - 15k to 25k (800 to 1500sqft)

b. Electricity bill - 5k to 20k (higher side if AC fitted)

c. Cleaning and Maintenance - 5k

Variable Expenses -

a. Trainers at 8k per month (max 3)

b. Marketing and Merchandising - 5k per month.

2) think about conducting a competitors analysis

In Pune only one Personal Studio stands out which is Master Trainer and has good relation with K and backed by K in getting clientele.

There are many good Personal Trainers like A having high paying clientele in the market and most of them are either connected with Golds and other big gyms, very few actually have their own Studios and most are unheard of. Being connected to big gyms means being hit by Covid lockdown but a good amount of online and offline clients at reduced fees.

Plenty of rich kids entering the fitness industry who have no career prospect but to invest in their own gym studios because they don't have the tendency to work under someone else.

Very few Personal Training Studios in existence. Establishing a set up is a costly affair, work is hectic and returns from gyms are seasonal, risk factor in gyms is high with day today management being required.

Being a big deal in fitness takes time and to get the required clientele marketing and credibility is required.

Personal Training Studios on big scale has not done by anyone and can't be done by anyone, Jcan make a set up but cannot groom anyone, K can groom but cannot give business to anyone unless and until you make K your God.

PT Studios is the new thing and unexplored business prospect in India.

3) think about doing a sensitivity analysis (what happens in the worst case scenario, what happens in an extremely good scenario, what happens in a breakeven scenario)

Worst Case Scenario - Lack of clientele.

How to tackle?

Be Flexible and Adaptive, Upgrade knowledge, have multiple expertise, have camera presence, be good at drafting programs and presentations. Most important thing is to collaborate with others doing different things in fitness and nutrition.

Good Scenario - steady flow of clients both online and offline

How to keep climbing the ladder?

Upgrade knowledge, gather new skill sets, network and collaborate, your speed determines your success, don't be complacent. Re-invent and Transform yourself. Networking and collaborating brings new clients and gives you the credibility that is needed.

Breakeven Scenario -

Trainer or operator is under achieving.

4) try to answer why somebody would buy a personal studio from us when they can do it themselves ?

It is easy to set up a "set up" but a different ball game running it. We will provide the backend support needed for holding up a business and our experience of many years and expert knowledge is something that no manufacturing company nor any teaching academy offers.

"Image is everything, everything is Image."

5) do you feel this need for one on one will increase or decrease ?

One on one will increase, people are in desperate need to fix their health be it body or mind or both. Personal attention is a must. A personal trainer is not just someone who takes exercise but is someone who looks after overall well being of the client. Spending an hour with someone every other day and focusing on personal well being makes the client share personal things. People are looking for someone to take care of them and to address their insecurities and currently the world is full of successful yet inwardly insecure people.

6) will this model work if we plan to operate on the lowest possible fee 6,000? for alternate days and 10,000? for 6 days a week ? If yes how ? If no, how do we tweak the model ?

It can work at 6k to 10k range but that is completely dependent upon the trainer and his/her aspirations. Everybody starts low but there is the art of selling expensive PTs which comes with confidence and knowledge. (It is all about selling actually, you can sell to many at lower rates and to a few at higher rates) No need to tweak our model as we are already the lowest to quote. Something not in our control as of now is the Olympic

Plates and Quality barbells (S is good and cheaper for Olympic plates while B barbells are best in the market) The overall feel of these things makes the difference.

Advanced thought process expected from you:

1) how can this model stand out?

No manufacturer nor teaching academy is offering this business model.

Studio model - lower costs, back end support both marketing and knowledge. We are not just setting up the Legacy Brand but we will be making the owner/trainer as a brand in the market.

2) what is your usp

Low cost

social media marketing course and tools

knowledge Certification

Grooming

quarterly back end support.

3) why should people enroll in your studio ?

Science backed training, result oriented, exercise and nutrition expertise. Ambience. The experience is based on teaching techniques, how well spoken and knowledgeable the coach is and ambience.

4) what experience delivery are you talking about to the customer ?

One on one coaching, target specific approach, knowledge share and documentation of individual client.

5) how will this model benefit the company

Machine/franchise sale and Brand Power. Proper Enforceable Legal Contracts. People want to fall in love be it a person or a brand, we don't just make one but we will make in thousands. Fitness is show business and we will put up a show which brings in more investors and equity. Re-inventing is the key.

6) why should anyone pay franchise fee ? How do you create value ?

Make them legally binding but make them pay out of love and respect and if they stop paying then take action which we have never done before.

Value - we teach them everything and teaching should be a brainwash. Take a look at most of the K students and how narrow minded they are. Give them an initial experience which can never be forgotten. Make the brand a craze, glamour it and people will be fans.

Our brand value lies in how we value it and enforce it. We are offering something that no one is offering as of yet.

K has tried it's hands at setting up studios but they didn't go well because there is no control of his on manufacturing and manufacturing expertise. Even F failed at commercial gym because of over achieving and zero gym management experience.

Personal Training Studios is a new prospect with absolutely no players in the field.

CHAPTER TWO

Nutrition For Her

A female body goes through many changes at various stages of life.

Stages

Age 13 to 16 puberty

Age 16 to 21 adolescent

Age 25 to 30 metabolism drops

Age 30 onwards muscle loss and calcium malabsorption (even if didn't go through pregnancy)

Age 40 onwards menopause sets in.

Even the menses take a toll on the body leading to iron deficiency and other mineral deficiencies which put the body and mind out of homeostasis. The menses also cause a lot of hormonal fluctuations which lead to body composition changes and habits.

Estrogen being the female hormone acts more towards relaxation and keeping the body soft and the way a girl should be. The very low testosterone levels which is how it is meant to be for women keeps muscle mass at a lower side leading to weight and fat gain easily with age.

A woman's body is a far more complex system when compared to the utilitarian male body, and this complexity itself makes women the wonderful caring and understanding beings that they are. Women are far more mentally strong than men but only if they take care of their health and fitness.

In Nutrition for Her we focus on these above aspects and tackle the various health issues faced by Her/You.

PCOD/PCOS

PCOD - Immature or partially matured eggs being released which turn into cyst.

Symptoms - acne, fatigue, irregular period, weight gain, facial or body hair, mood swings.

PCOS - higher level of androgens (male hormones) produced by ovaries. Interrupt egg formation and release. Eggs turn into cyst (sacs filled with liquid)

Symptoms - metabolic problems, obesity, irregular or no menstrual cycle, chronic fatigue, brain fog, hair thinning and abnormal body hair growth.

Causes of PCOD/PCOS - no scientific specific reason. Purely lifestyle disease.

Diet to follow -

Limit sugar intake.

Avoid processed foods.

Avoid junk and street food.

Protein rich diet as per requirement. Too much not good.

Focus on nutrition density rather than calorie deficit.

Exercise is a must when it comes to dealing with PCOD/PCOs as it reduces stress and controls mood swings leading to healthy habits and lifestyle.

2. Thyroid

Thyroid gland produces hormones which regulate body's metabolic rate controlling heart, muscle and digestive function, brain development and bone maintenance.

Thyroid disease is a condition wherein your thyroid gland is not able to produce the right amount of hormones.

Hypothyroidism - not enough hormones produced

Symptoms- dry hair and skin, slow heartbeat, fatigue, heavy periods, weight gain, muscle pains, constipation

Hyperthyroidism - weight loss, hair loss, faster heartbeat, muscle weakness, difficulty sleeping, frequent bowel movements, scant periods, irritability

Diet - structured differently for both.

Exercise is a must.

Pregnancy

Planning which is pre-pregnancy -

With lifestyle disorders like pcod/pcos and obesity or below normal weight, women have a hard time getting pregnant or not able to maintain the pregnancy because of complications. Health and fitness are very important when it comes to getting pregnant as well as for having healthy children.

Actual Pregnancy- Pregnancy is divided into 3 trimester and every trimester requires special care and alterations to the diet and exercise. Consumption of food and the activities consuming your energy will mold your child.

Post natal - Your body has gone through a tremendous strain and stress not just during the delivery but throughout the pregnancy period. These changes were beneficial for the baby and you, but now it is about you and you taking care of your baby so there are changes required for diet as well as exercise.

Weight Loss and women - Like said before, various stages as per age and the dominant female hormone make women prone to fat and weight gain with less toned muscles. Creating a better understanding of your body with you, will help not just to lose fat but will make you more confident and strong. Calorie deficit is not the only way forward as some women starve but still no weight loss. Energy expenditure is high and still no weight loss. Why? We tailor make the program for you.

Mental Wellness - Rejuvenate and nourish with food. Exercise is the mind body connection in action leading to better self awareness and a healthy lifestyle.

Nutrition for Her is all about your relationship with food and movement. It is to help you and guide you through your fitness journey or let's say the journey of life.

CHAPTER THREE

Services explanation module

How to explain the services?

Greetings,

I hope I have not called you in the busy moment, as I have an investment proposition for you in terms of health and well- being.

"Target response"

No, I am definitely not selling you any insurance policy here, but I am calling from The Human Excellence Network just to know if you are doing fine in terms of health and mental well-being and if you are happy in the general sense of terms.

" "

We at The Human Excellence Network are here to listen and I am making this call to help you in the best possible of ways.

" "

The whole idea of finding answers or of making life better is through the way of MINDFULNESS. The word mindfulness means to become aware.

" "

The Human Excellence Network has the primary code called THE MINDFUL PROGRAM and the approach is H.U.M.A.N

H – Health

U – Understanding

M – Movement

A – Awareness and

N – Nourishment

" "

If you would like to know more

Yes – continue

NO – How about I call you some other time suitable for you and in the meantime forward you the details on mail or on your WhatsApp number? (even if no still send the details)

Yes – continue

What makes us truly happy? Our friends, our family, our fun time. How about "we make our own happiness" being happy and feeling good from the inside. What do you think?"

" "

Life has its ups and downs and if someone is saying Life is all good is just trying to sell you something and investing is the new price, but it brings in good results and that is what we do here at The Human Excellence Network.

" "

Well, we have various programs and courses that will not only benefit you in terms of health and well-being but shall also help you in your career and personal life goals.

" "

The various programs we have, fall under 3 basic categories and we have tie-ups with multiple brands which are here to cater for you and those categories are

a. Education and Knowledge
b. Training and Exercise
c. Food and Nourishment
What would be your choice?
" "

Education and Knowledge involves courses on Exercise Science and Food Science which will not only help you understand yourself better as to your relationship with food and movement but also help you in building a career in the fitness industry.

Training and Exercise is powered by H and DEN which are online as well as offline exercise programs be it for losing weight or getting fitter.

H is about making exercise fun and intense while THE DEN is all about hard-core technique oriented physical training.

We make sure that you stay motivated and focused by our approach in the training and you having fun while exploring your strengths and overcoming your weaknesses. It is all about going for the new high.

Food and nourishment is under the guidance of "GET FIT WITH NIK" which has a personalised approach to food habits and diet which are customised to your needs and goals and also addressing any health issues that you may be facing and our tagline is "Nurture and Rejuvenate with Food."

We all love to eat food and in GET FIT WITH NIK we help you build your relationship with food. It is ALL ABOUT FOOD AND YOU. If you happen to be staying in Pune, we also have meals provided by our food partner "T" which provides healthy meals at your doorstep.

How would you like to proceed and which service would be your preference?

" "

Actions - Send the Forms to fill up

Our forms are designed so that you spend some time with your own self and answer the questions which are close to your mind, body, heart and soul. Your answers are safe with us and we maintain a fiduciary relationship with our clients because we believe in personal relations and the importance of one's privacy, like a doctor patient relationship. We THE HUMAN EXCELLENCE NETWORK ARE HERE TO LISTEN and we shall do the follow ups necessary for your needs. It is a network for you.

Good day and take care.

SEE YOU THEN.

CHAPTER FOUR

Mindfulness Program

The whole idea of finding answers or of making life better is through the way of MINDFULNESS. The word mindfulness means to become aware.
" "

The Human Excellence Network has the primary code called THE MINDFUL PROGRAM and the approach is H.U.M.A.N
H – Health
U – Understanding
M – Movement
A – Awareness and
N – Nourishment
- Self-Reflection - Self-Awareness - Self-Realization
The Human Excellence Network has the primary code called THE MINDFULLNESS PROGRAM and the approach is H.U.M.A.N

Health is a state of complete physical and mental well-being and not merely the absence of disease or infirmity.

Understanding to listen, to know. to build self-awareness through self-reflection and helping you understand your relationship with food, movement, habits, mind, peace and heart.

Movement is a state of motion of the body and the mind. With customized exercise regime, you will be able to redevelop and engage the mind muscle connection and discover a new you.

Awareness of thy mind, body, heart and soul. It is in the moments of calm and storm that you meet yourself and build a better you.

Nourishment is what you consume, nourishes you. Be mindful of not just the food you eat but also as to what your mind consumes and releases. Nourishment of the 5 senses.

It's a state of mind.

Mindfulness is the basic human ability to be fully present, aware of where we are and what we're doing, and not overly reactive or overwhelmed by what's going on around us.

It can be cultivated through proven techniques.

Here are some examples: Seated, walking, standing, and moving meditation; Short pauses we insert into everyday life; Merging meditation practice with other activities, such as yoga or sports.

It's good for you.

When we're mindful, we reduce stress, enhance performance, gain insight and awareness through observing our own mind, and increase our attention to others' well-being.

But it's not all in your head.

Meditation begins and ends in the body. It involves taking the time to pay attention to where we are and what's going on, and that starts with being aware of our body.

When we practice mindfulness, we're practicing the art of creating space for ourselves—space to think, space to breathe, space between ourselves and our reactions.

A friendly reminder: We've done our research, but you should, too! Check our sources against your own, and always exercise sound judgement.

Sources:

"What Is Mindfulness?" Mindful, 18 Feb. 2021, www.mindful.org/what-is-mindfulness. "How to Practice Mindfulness." Mindful, 24 Sept. 2020, www.mindful.org/how-to-practice-mindfulness.

The mindfulness program is devised by Nikhil Maduskar which is a ninety day program which involves google forms, google sheets of diet, exercise, activity sheet and others. The program is tailor made to help the individual achieve a quality of life and self awareness.

CHAPTER FIVE

The Human Excellence Network

THE HUMAN EXCELLENCE NETWORK BUSINESS PLAN A.I

A. What is the mission and vision of the organization?

Mission –
Our mission is to help mankind in achieving its true potential by providing a platform to improve health and knowledge by following a holistic approach towards life and living it.

Vision –
The vision of our organisation is to create a platform for collaborating excellence from the field of nutrition, fitness science, healthcare, computer technology, software, artificial intelligence and spirituality for promoting human excellence and progress by catering to the holistic development of the individual in the society and help our customer/member to achieve his/her true potential. When the mind, body and spirit is taken care of then the eco-system for progressive development is established.

A. What is the product or service? How will it evolve as a family of products and services?

Product A – Knowledge, training and education in the field of nutrition and fitness science.

Fitness science encompasses nutrition, kinesiology, biomechanics, physiotherapy, medicine, psychology, neuroscience and human performance.

Service A – Counselling and training programs in exercise, nutrition, mental wellbeing, wellness and spirituality.

Product A evolution – knowledge creation in both physical (print) and digital format and being taught, trained and researched in order to promote and impart real knowledge to bring about professionals to deliver an eco-system for human health and performance. From certification courses to diplomas to degrees and beyond. We teach to create thinkers and researchers and not just service providers. The developments in technology and software and artificial intelligence can help us create products or further develop those products which are already present in the market.

Service A evolution – developing the existing methods and systems of counselling, training and diagnosis which can evaluate the overall health of an individual/customer and provide sustainable solutions for good health and human performance.

Product B – Digital Platform (global)

Product C – App (global)

C. What is the competitive landscape? How are other leading players serving the market? What trends do market research and analyst reports indicate?

Competitive Landscape Regional India – Pan India presence is held by 3 institutes which are K11 Fitness Science Academy, Institute of Nutrition and Fitness Science (INFS by Fittr) and Boss Academy. All these and their courses are accredited to international bodies and Skill

India but not recognised as educational institutes by The National Assessment and Accreditation Council (NAAC). There is not a single institute to get such a recognition nor is the authority on Fitness Science as their training module and course material is curated material having true source from ISSA (International Sports Sciences Association). Localized to Pune, currently there is Bodywizard which is working with Lighthouse (NGO) to impart knowledge regarding personal training and nutrition. Lighthouse has a copy of our course material both in hard and soft copy and the possibility of misuse can be there but then most work in this field is derivative.

Price range of any of these courses varies from 7k to 100k and many have shifted to online platforms. Online does not truly provide a full hand on training which is required to make professionals.

International Market – ISSA, NASM, Shaw Academy, Squat University and many more Academies are there which are teaching these courses and many are developed by experts from the fitness industry.

The noteworthy and inspiring Institute is Pre-Script which is an online company based outside of India and is an online platform with their coaches conducting offline classes in their respective countries. They have a vast pool of experienced knowledgeable trainers providing various courses in fitness and human performance.

Market Research on Fitness Industry – India is developing at a fast clip and competitive lifestyle has led to increased stress levels. Anxiety, depression, high blood pressure, and lack of sleep are common even among the Gen X and this has given way to the rise of the wellness industry.

According to a study by McKinsey & Company the wellness industry is currently valued at $1.5 trillion globally. This study analysing 7,500 consumers in 6 countries (including India) has offered key insights into consumer behaviour. The consumer trends in this study can be grouped into the following broad categories: -

HEALTH: People are investing in many remote medical devices that can constantly monitor their state of well-being. With the increase in popularity in digital wearables, telemedicine, and remote patient monitoring services, this trend is bound to increase.

NUTRITION: Dieting has always been a significant part of being healthy. An increase in dietary food, supplements, and nutrition coaches has been observed in recent years.

FITNESS: People are exercising more whether it's jogging, going to the gym, investing in a Pedometer etc.

MINDFULLNESS: Introspection, understanding the body and its processes to the molecular level, and figuring out ways to implement clarity of thought and methods for improving focus have been huge draws for the wellness industry. Further, with central government's schemes like AYUSH and the introduction of International Yoga Day by the United Nations, this particular trend has seen enormous growth.

CHANGING TRENDS OF THE INDIAN WELLNESS INDUSTRY

Spurt in Organic Products: India has become one of the largest producers of organic products. A growing number of people are actively investing monthly in organically grown produce, organically processed meat, wood-pressed or cold-pressed oil, cosmetics made from organic materials, and clothes made from pure cotton instead of manufactured materials. People becoming more conscious of what they put in their bodies has led to a steady increase in organic shops across India.

Healthcare goes Phyigital: Apart from physical chemist stores, there has been an increase in popularity of telemedicine and remote-patient monitoring. Consequently, healthcare and the wellness industry are gaining an increased online presence. There is a plethora of online exercise videos, fitness and meditation apps which have flooded the internet space.

Increased Physical Activity and Nutritional Supplements: From using simple calcium supplements and energy drinks to adhering to a strict diet regimen, today's consumers are genuinely worried about falling sick, which has led to an increase in purchasing supplements.

Consumers have started buying Vitamin, Zinc, and Iron tablets to whip up their immunity. Indians have also begun consuming Gluten free cereals, cold-pressed juices, Avocados, and other food products recommended to be healthier alternatives.

Voice of Social Media Influencers: With the increase in online dependence, the voice of social media influencers is soon to be gospel when it comes to maintaining a fit body and healthy mind. Much like how mainstream celebrities endorse various products, the wellness industry has seen great rewards in deploying online influencers to support their products.

India has become a wellness hub globally with a 12 per cent growth per annum. The Make in India thrust will bring in more investments in this sector. The government has earmarked a budget of around Rs 3,400 crore for the next 5 years to set up and strengthen Ayush Wellness Centres under the National Ayush Mission. This has sparked a rise in start-ups in the wellness sector.

Undoubtedly, the global pandemic has given rise to a new consumer behaviour where they are becoming more conscious about their well-being and choosing a lifestyle which is sustainable and healthy.

The aftermath of the pandemic has resulted in increased implementation of technology, and with the acceptance in the consumer market in India, the wellness industry will evolve and grow further.

Home gyms: According to a recent poll of 2,000 people by OnePoll, 75% of people believe it's easier to stay fit at home. Since the COVID-19 pandemic began in early 2020, 64% of respondents stated that they're more interested in at-home exercise than ever before. As the uncertainty of the pandemic continues, it's anticipated that most people will stick with at-home workouts, dedicating living space to personalized home gyms. Notably, you can get in a good workout without needing to buy expensive equipment. The average American spent $95.79 on home gym equipment during quarantine considerably less than a gym membership. With a pair of dumbbells and exercise bands, you can make getting in shape accessible and affordable.

Apps for minimal-equipment exercise: Though using a home gym works for some people, many don't have enough space. What's more, it's possible to get in a good workout without spending a penny. Going forward, expect to see more people utilizing free YouTube videos and exercise apps to guide them through workouts. Many of these exercises require minimal or no equipment and use your body weight for resistance.

Free exercise apps include:

Asana Rebel

This app provides fitness, nutrition, and wellness tips and advice at no cost, though a pro version is available for purchase.

Nike Training Club

With almost 200 workouts to choose from, this app is the perfect solution for those looking for a good workout with minimal to no equipment required.

Nike Run Club

This training app is designed for those looking to step up their running game. Providing distance challenges, daily motivation, GPS tracking, and customized coaching plans, it's perfect for beginner to intermediate runners.

Daily Yoga

This app provides hundreds of yoga poses and classes for all fitness levels. For a fee, you can upgrade to a pro version

Luxe indoor gyms

Gym and boutique fitness studio closures during the pandemic led to a surge in sales of high-end workout equipment. In fact, the treadmill and stationary bike company Peloton experienced a 232% increase in sales during the first quarter of 2020. Though these exercise machines require an initial investment, they're hugely popular and highly rated. Affluent customers are expected to create customized, fully equipped home gyms replete with items like high-end treadmills, stationary bikes, row machines, and workout mirrors.

High-end workout equipment and smart gyms include:

Peloton Bike and Peloton Bike+

Peloton bikes offer a wide range of features, such as built-in speakers and an HD touchscreen with thousands of interactive classes.

The Mirror

This smart gym is a screen that functions as a personal trainer while it's in use and a stylish mirror when it's off. It boasts an array of workouts, including tai chi, yoga, boxing, and targeted strength training.

Tonal

This digital weight system features built-in resistance up to 200 pounds (90 kg), using electromagnetic resistance to give you a powerful workout without the need for weights.

Holistic fitness: Due to a surge in interest in whole-body health, many people are approaching fitness as one piece of a larger health puzzle rather than a way to simply gain strength. To that end, they're balancing exercise with restorative activities like sleep and meditation.

D.   In what way will we be different? Why should someone buy my products or services?

Knowledge – Everybody else is trying to sell saying they are right and others are wrong when it comes to nutrition and training while all of them know that applied nutrition is not an exact science and varies from individual to individual when it comes to implementation. Most of the exercise models focus on gym exercises and creates variations to justify their authority. We step out of this smoke and mirror and deliver real knowledge and represent it as it is and teach how to apply the same. We create an in depth course/knowledge material and grade as per university standards and collaborate and have on board all professionals not just from sports and fitness fields but from the medical practitioners' field along with scientists dealing with the brain, biology and microbiology. First step is to get Skill India and International accreditation and go for the Education Board Recognition in order to become an authority in the field of fitness science.

Service – Counselling and Training Programs – Personalized approach addressing the real needs of the customer and providing solutions not just to improve health parameters but also improve overall wellbeing and performance. Provide health condition specific or therapeutic diets and training programs. Focus more on women health and wellbeing. How do we cater to our targeted audience? It is by first knowing and understanding the functioning of the body, hormones and thinking patterns or psychology. Multiple buyer personas to be identified. Habits and routines help us to identify buyer personas. This creates the need of presenting and delivering our service in variety and target specific rather than following a single format.

Why Should someone buy from us?

Every individual requires empathy, understanding and, a structure benefiting the individual's ecosystem which is his/her mind, body, heart and soul with an extended horizon encompassing personal and professional relationships and aspirations. The Human Excellence Network is the individual centric platform to help the said individual to bring out a better version by working on own self by the methods of self-exploration, self-realization and self-awareness.

E. How will I get my first paying customer? How will I price my goods and services?

First Paying Customer – by marketing and word of mouth. The brand and its conceptualization will attract customers.

Pricing – As per market rates and competitively positioned. No discounting.

F. What will be the Marketing Strategy?

1.To utilize all avenues of digital media and social media platforms such as Facebook, Instagram, medium, LinkedIn, our own websites and other platforms to share knowledge and content via articles and blogs.

2. Conducting Awareness Programs and Workshops at school, colleges, corporate events and to identify every potential platform to put our voice out.

3. Conducting Social Welfare Programs and Camps for the health and well-being of the society. Not only spreading knowledge but also joy and happiness as that is the major aspect of well-being.

4. Merchandize and kits.

5. Print

6. To hire social media marketing consultants and hire third party agencies.

G. What organizational structure will I need? What critical skills do the founders possess and which one needs to be supplemented.

H. What capital expenditure will be needed and why? How have I determined the adequacy and cost?

a. Basic Digital Infra 2,00,000/-
b. App 10,00,000/-

I. What revenue expenditure will be needed for same period.

Total expense year one -
a. Salaries 10,00,000/-
b. Marketing 3,00,000/-
c. Technology 2,00,000/-
d. Merchandize 2,00,000/-
e. Travel 1,00,000/-
f. Misc. 2,00,000/-
Total 20,00,000/-
Office Space 6,00,000/- rental

J. How is my cost structure different from that of the competition?

a. We are spending more on skilled resource in a way to support knowledge creation and delivery.
b. Balancing out expenses for both offline and online branding activities.
c. Merchandize for promotion as well as sale.
d. Digital infra to be an avenue of revenue generation.

K. What is my 3-year cash flow?

Year 1 Revenue
Programs 1,50,000/- per month
Training 50,000/- per month
Education 3,00,000/- per month
Total 5,00,000/- per month
Y.O.Y Growth @ 15%
Excluding Mobile App and merchandize and other product development.

AX. When will the organization break even?

18 months from first capital input.

ALL. What is the funding plan? Personal Capital, Venture funding and Loans.

All three options to be utilized. Take the company to an IPO 3 years down the line. Initial Structuration of the company to be done in a way which encourages investment and wealth creation.

N. What is the plan for recruitment, training and retention of people?

Selection Criteria for Recruitment

- Educational Qualification – Graduate and above. English proficiency. Multiple languages.
- Work Experience and life experience.
- Passionate towards making a difference for human development. Broad vision.
- Knowledge of the human body and performance.
- Technical expertise – nutrition, psychology, computers, coding knowledge, designing, medical, anatomy, emotional intelligence and business management.
- Hobbies – reading.

Training – vision, mission, basics of knowledge to be part of T.H.E.N, business and communications, any specified skill set or knowledge beneficial for the progress of the organization.

Retention – recruitment process.

- What are the R & D plans? How will the activity be sustained over time?

R&D avenues –

1. Knowledge creation and implementation with delivery – continuous process
2. Training Methods – evolving process
3. Software and Digital Infra – Apps, websites, software, etc. – third party collaborations.
4. Artificial Intelligence – in house blue print and development.
5. Products – digital products in wearables, physical and tangible merchandise, trigger products.
6. Integration of A.I for medical treatment. – in house (3 years down the line)

P. What are the manufacturing and distribution plans?

We are into creating knowledge content and delivery – online in digital format and offline in print format. For offline we already have publications, publishers and printers.

Distribution channel is to utilize digital infrastructure and social media. We have the following domains under us –

www.mindhacknfsi.com
www.thehumanexcellencenetwork.com
www.getfitwithnik.co.in
and their respective Facebook and Instagram handles.

Q. What are the various risks involved in building the organization?

The various risks involved are as follows –

   i. Hiring and retaining the right kind of employees.
  ii. Initial cash flows and building up clientele.
 iii. Time factor and perseverance (need team and staff to be vision centric and proactive)
 iv. Back end support to every department.
  v. Market penetration and awareness.
 vi. Fund Allocation and financial management.

R. In what way will the team de-risk those?

   i. Right kind of employees – the way there is a buyer persona, we will have the employee persona who aligns with our thought process, vision and aspirations with some technical expertise beneficial or complementary to existing team and is highly educated and open to new ideas and change. – Recruitment Process Head

  ii. Initial Cash flows and clientele – Cash flow to be controlled at all times, not to spend unnecessarily on marketing. Appointing a financial management consultant and aligning expenses with goals to be achieved and set for quarterly targets. Budget allocation. – Head of Business and Communication

 iii. Time factor – set defined goals for the vision, departments and individual team member to be achieved in a specified time frame. – Strategist

 iv. Back end support – Developing and defining the connectivity and complimentary structure of every department and individual. – Head of Business and

Communication

v. Market penetration and awareness – connecting with people and organizations and putting out the message as to who we are what we do and what we aim to achieve. – Head of Business and Communication

vi. Fund Allocation and financial management – budgets. – President of the Company/Chairman of the Board.

Monday, 08 August 2022
NIKHIL MADUSKAR
Founder, The Human Excellence Network
A.I

CHAPTER SIX

THENTECH LIFESTYLE

BUSINESS PLAN

A. What is the mission and vision of the organization?

Mission –
Our mission is to help mankind in achieving its true potential by providing a platform to improve health and knowledge by following a holistic approach towards life and living it.

Vision –
The vision of our organisation is to create a platform for collaborating excellence from the field of nutrition, fitness science, healthcare, computer technology, software, artificial intelligence and spirituality for promoting human excellence and progress by catering to the holistic development of the individual in the society and help our customer/member to achieve his/her true potential. When the mind, body and spirit is taken care of then the eco-system for progressive development is established.

THENTECH has adopted this mission and vision from THE HUMAN EXCELLENCE NETWORK and in pursuit of the above ideologies, THENTECH shall be the real Software and Technology Development Company. While THEN remains a source of inspiration and the bible of core values in developing the THENTECH technologies.

A. What is the product or service? How will it evolve as a family of products and services?

PRIMARY - We move ahead by getting together our very own software and technology set up which will be into developing websites, web apps, mobile apps, software and other technology needs of our own in house apps which will be made available in the open market for customer engagement and service.

The said software development team shall also be engaged in developing applications and software for third parties which makes an additional revenue stream for THENTECH.

Approach A – Knowledge, training and education in the field of nutrition and fitness science.

Fitness science encompasses nutrition, kinesiology, biomechanics, physiotherapy, medicine, psychology, neuroscience and human performance.

Approach B – Counselling and training programs in exercise, nutrition, mental wellbeing, wellness and spirituality.

Approach A evolution – knowledge creation in both physical (print) and digital format and being taught, trained and researched in order to promote and impart real knowledge to bring about professionals to deliver an eco-system for human health and performance. From certification courses to diplomas to degrees and beyond. We teach to create thinkers and researchers and not just service providers. The developments in technology and software and artificial intelligence can help us create products or further develop those products which are already present in the market.

Approach B evolution – developing the existing methods and systems of counselling, training and diagnosis which can evaluate the overall health of an individual/ customer and provide sustainable solutions for good health and human performance.

Product A – THENTECH Mobile Applications/Web Apps/ Websites (global)

Project A – **Tiffico App**

Food is the necessity of life and the existing players cater to restaurants and customers whereas TIFFICO shall engage in the service of connecting Tiffin providers with the customers.

Even today students, office goers and many more prefer home-made food consisting of Dabbas having roti sabzi and Daal rice as they are the staple foods of India and stomach filling as well as affordable.

An app which caters to the needs of the students, office goers and the tiffin providers.

We take upon us the responsibility of creating women empowerment and women entrepreneurship with our slogan "ONE WOMAN, ONE KITCHEN" The Cloud Kitchens of the Technological Age with focus on providing employment and earning for women.

Project B – **THENFIT/WEVOLVE App** (global)

Application both on android and IOs for fitness, nutrition, health and mental wellness.

- Training
- Counselling

- Nutrition Programs
- BMI and Calorie counter/ tracker
- Other devices connectivity – smart watch, body analysis scale.

Project C – THEN Academy of Fitness Science and Nutrition Website. (global)

Edtech Website for Fitness Science and Nutrition covering original course material with Live and Recorded Classes.

Project D – **Athletes App**

Sports and Sporting Events App – Seasons, Trainings, Physiotherapists, Nutrition and Coaches on one platform. (Indian Railways and Army has a major say in sporting activities in India) Khelo India.

Product B – Devices

The software will be developed simultaneously with the above application development. Products range from Body analysis machine to a smart watch. The manufacturing can be done from third party while we hold and own the patents for the same.

C. What is the competitive landscape? How are other leading players serving the market? What trends do market research and analyst reports indicate?

Competitive Landscape Regional India – Pan India presence is held by 3 institutes which are K11 Fitness Science Academy, Institute of Nutrition and Fitness Science (INFS by Fittr), Fittr and Boss Academy. All these and their courses are accredited to international bodies and Skill India but not recognised as educational institutes by The National Assessment and Accreditation Council

(NAAC). There is not a single institute to get such a recognition nor is the authority on Fitness Science as their training module and course material is curated material having true source from ISSA (International Sports Sciences Association). Localized to Pune, currently there is Bodywizard which is working with Lighthouse (NGO) to impart knowledge regarding personal training and nutrition. Lighthouse has a copy of our course material both in hard and soft copy and the possibility of misuse can be there but then most work in this field is derivative.

Price range of any of these courses varies from 7k to 100k and many have shifted to online platforms. Online does not truly provide a full hand on training which is required to make professionals.

International Market – ISSA, NASM, Shaw Academy, Squat University and many more Academies are there which are teaching these courses and many are developed by experts from the fitness industry.

The noteworthy and inspiring Institute is Pre-Script which is an online company based outside of India and is an online platform with their coaches conducting offline classes in their respective countries. They have a vast pool of experienced knowledgeable trainers providing various courses in fitness and human performance.

Market Research on Fitness Industry – India is developing at a fast clip and competitive lifestyle has led to increased stress levels. Anxiety, depression, high blood pressure, and lack of sleep are common even among the Gen X and this has given way to the rise of the wellness industry.

According to a study by McKinsey & Company the wellness industry is currently valued at $1.5 trillion globally. This study analysing 7,500 consumers in 6 countries (including India) has offered key insights into consumer behaviour. The consumer trends in this study can be grouped into the following broad categories: -

HEALTH: People are investing in many remote medical devices that can constantly monitor their state of well-being. With the increase in popularity in digital wearables, telemedicine, and remote patient monitoring services, this trend is bound to increase.

NUTRITION: Dieting has always been a significant part of being healthy. An increase in dietary food, supplements, and nutrition coaches has been observed in recent years.

FITNESS: People are exercising more whether it's jogging, going to the gym, investing in a Pedometer etc.

MINDFULLNESS: Introspection, understanding the body and its processes to the molecular level, and figuring out ways to implement clarity of thought and methods for improving focus have been huge draws for the wellness industry. Further, with central government's schemes like AYUSH and the introduction of International Yoga Day by the United Nations, this particular trend has seen enormous growth.

CHANGING TRENDS OF THE INDIAN WELLNESS INDUSTRY

Spurt in Organic Products: India has become one of the largest producers of organic products. A growing number of people are actively investing monthly in organically grown produce, organically processed meat, wood-pressed or cold-pressed oil, cosmetics made from organic materials, and clothes made from pure cotton instead of manufactured materials. People becoming more conscious of what they put in their bodies has led to a steady increase in organic shops across India.

Healthcare goes Phyigital: Apart from physical chemist stores, there has been an increase in popularity of telemedicine and remote-patient monitoring. Consequently, healthcare and the wellness industry are gaining an increased online presence. There is a plethora of online exercise videos, fitness and meditation apps which have flooded the internet space.

Increased Physical Activity and Nutritional Supplements: From using simple calcium supplements and energy drinks to adhering to a strict diet regimen, today's consumers are genuinely worried about falling sick, which has led to an increase in purchasing supplements.

Consumers have started buying Vitamin, Zinc, and Iron tablets to whip up their immunity. Indians have also begun consuming Gluten free cereals, cold-pressed juices, Avocados, and other food products recommended to be healthier alternatives.

Voice of Social Media Influencers: With the increase in online dependence, the voice of social media influencers is soon to be gospel when it comes to maintaining a fit body and healthy mind. Much like how mainstream celebrities endorse various products, the wellness industry has seen great rewards in deploying online influencers to support their products.

India has become a wellness hub globally with a 12 per cent growth per annum. The Make in India thrust will bring in more investments in this sector. The government has earmarked a budget of around Rs 3,400 crore for the next 5 years to set up and strengthen Ayush Wellness Centres under the National Ayush Mission. This has sparked a rise in start-ups in the wellness sector.

Undoubtedly, the global pandemic has given rise to a new consumer behaviour where they are becoming more conscious about their well-being and choosing a lifestyle which is sustainable and healthy.

The aftermath of the pandemic has resulted in increased implementation of technology, and with the acceptance in the consumer market in India, the wellness industry will evolve and grow further.

Home gyms: According to a recent poll of 2,000 people by OnePoll, 75% of people believe it's easier to stay fit at home. Since the COVID-19 pandemic began in early 2020, 64% of respondents stated that they're more interested in at-home exercise than ever before. As the uncertainty of the pandemic continues, it's anticipated that most people will stick with at-home workouts, dedicating living space to personalized home gyms. Notably, you can get in a good workout without needing to buy expensive equipment. The average American spent $95.79 on home gym equipment during quarantine considerably less than a gym membership. With a pair of dumbbells and exercise bands, you can make getting in shape accessible and affordable.

Apps for minimal-equipment exercise: Though using a home gym works for some people, many don't have enough space. What's more, it's possible to get in a good workout without spending a penny. Going forward, expect to see more people utilizing free YouTube videos and exercise apps to guide them through workouts. Many of these exercises require minimal or no equipment and use your body weight for resistance.

Free exercise apps include:

Asana Rebel

This app provides fitness, nutrition, and wellness tips and advice at no cost, though a pro version is available for purchase.

Nike Training Club

With almost 200 workouts to choose from, this app is the perfect solution for those looking for a good workout with minimal to no equipment required.

Nike Run Club

This training app is designed for those looking to step up their running game. Providing distance challenges, daily motivation, GPS tracking, and customized coaching plans, it's perfect for beginner to intermediate runners.

Daily Yoga

This app provides hundreds of yoga poses and classes for all fitness levels. For a fee, you can upgrade to a pro version

Luxe indoor gyms

Gym and boutique fitness studio closures during the pandemic led to a surge in sales of high-end workout equipment. In fact, the treadmill and stationary bike company Peloton experienced a 232% increase in sales during the first quarter of 2020. Though these exercise machines require an initial investment, they're hugely popular and highly rated. Affluent customers are expected to create customized, fully equipped home gyms replete with items like high-end treadmills, stationary bikes, row machines, and workout mirrors.

High-end workout equipment and smart gyms include:

Peloton Bike and Peloton Bike+

Peloton bikes offer a wide range of features, such as built-in speakers and an HD touchscreen with thousands of interactive classes.

The Mirror

This smart gym is a screen that functions as a personal trainer while it's in use and a stylish mirror when it's off. It boasts an array of workouts, including tai chi, yoga, boxing, and targeted strength training.

Tonal

This digital weight system features built-in resistance up to 200 pounds (90 kg), using electromagnetic resistance to give you a powerful workout without the need for weights.

Holistic fitness: Due to a surge in interest in whole-body health, many people are approaching fitness as one piece of a larger health puzzle rather than a way to simply gain strength. To that end, they're balancing exercise with restorative activities like sleep and meditation.

D. In what way will we be different? Why should someone buy my products or services?

A complete digital platform for Fitness, Nutrition and Health.

Knowledge – Everybody else is trying to sell saying they are right and others are wrong when it comes to nutrition and training while all of them know that applied nutrition is not an exact science and varies from individual to individual when it comes to implementation. Most of the exercise models focus on gym exercises and creates variations to justify their authority. We step out of this smoke and mirror and deliver real knowledge and represent it as it is and teach how to apply the same. We create an in depth course/knowledge material and grade as per university standards and collaborate and have on board all professionals not just from sports and fitness fields but from the medical practitioners' field along with scientists dealing with the brain, biology and microbiology. We get the necessary accreditations.

Service – Counselling and Training Programs – Personalized approach addressing the real needs of the customer and providing solutions not just to improve health parameters but also improve overall wellbeing and performance. Provide health condition specific or therapeutic diets and training programs. Focus more on women health and wellbeing. How do we cater to our targeted audience? It is by first knowing and understanding the functioning of the body, hormones and thinking patterns or psychology. Multiple buyer personas to be identified. Habits and routines help us to identify buyer personas. This creates the need of presenting and delivering our service in variety and target specific rather than following a single format.

Why Should someone buy from us?

Every individual requires empathy, understanding and, a structure benefiting the individual's ecosystem which is his/her mind, body, heart and soul with an extended horizon encompassing personal and professional relationships and aspirations. THENTECH will create an ecosystem of individual centric platform to help the said individual to bring out a better version by working on own self by the methods of self-exploration, self-realization and self-awareness.

E. How will I get my first paying customer? How will I price my goods and services?

First Paying Customer – by marketing and word of mouth. The brand and its conceptualization will attract customers.

Pricing – As per market rates and competitively positioned. No discounting.

F. What will be the Marketing Strategy?

1.To utilize all avenues of digital media and social media platforms such as Facebook, Instagram, medium, LinkedIn, our own websites and other platforms to share knowledge and content via articles and blogs.

2. Conducting Awareness Programs and Workshops at school, colleges, corporate events and to identify every potential platform to put our voice out.

3. Conducting Social Welfare Programs and Camps for the health and well-being of the society. Not only spreading knowledge but also joy and happiness as that is the major aspect of well-being.

4. Merchandize and kits.

5. Print

6. To hire social media marketing consultants and hire third party agencies.

G. What organizational structure will I need? What critical skills do the founders possess and which one needs to be supplemented.

H. What capital expenditure will be needed and why? How have I determined the adequacy and cost?

a. SYSTEMS INFRA 12,00,000/-
b. DEVELOPMENT 20,00,000/-

I. What revenue expenditure will be needed for same period.

Total expense year one -
a. Salaries 20,00,000/-
b. Marketing 10,00,000/-
d. Merchandize 3,00,000/-

e. Travel 5,00,000/-
f. Misc. 2,00,000/-
Total 40,00,000/-
Office Space 3,00,000/- rental

J. How is my cost structure different from that of the competition?

a. Developing the apps in house reduces development cost as well as maintenance cost of the apps.

b. We are spending more on skilled resource in a way to support knowledge and content creation and delivery.

c. Balancing out expenses for both offline and online branding activities.

d. Merchandize for promotion as well as sale.

e. Digital infra can be monetized for revenue generation.

K. What is my 3-year cash flow?

Year 1 Revenue from 4th month of starting operation
Programs through THENFIT APP 7,50,000/- per month
Training 1,50,000/- per month
Education 3,00,000/- per month
Third Party Product Development 3,00,000/- per month
Total 15,00,000/- per month
Y.O.Y Growth @ 15%
Excluding Mobile App Monetization and merchandize.
Applications are assets which have market value.

AX. When will the organization break even?

18 months from first capital input.

ALL. What is the funding plan? Personal Capital, Venture funding and Loans.

All three options to be utilized. Take the company to an IPO 3 years down the line. Initial Structuration of the company to be done in a way which encourages investment and wealth creation.

N. What is the plan for recruitment, training and retention of people?

Selection Criteria for Recruitment

- Educational Qualification – Graduate and above. English proficiency. Multiple languages.
- Work Experience and life experience.
- Passionate towards making a difference for human development. Broad vision.
- Knowledge of the human body and performance.
- Technical expertise – nutrition, psychology, computers, coding knowledge, designing, medical, anatomy, emotional intelligence and business management.
- Hobbies – reading.

Training – vision, mission, basics of knowledge to be part of T.H.E.N, business and communications, any specified skill set or knowledge beneficial for the progress of the organization.

Retention – recruitment process.

- What are the R & D plans? How will the activity be sustained over time?

R&D avenues –

1. Knowledge creation and implementation with delivery – continuous process
2. Training Methods – evolving process
3. Software and Digital Infra – Apps, websites, software, etc. – third party collaborations.
4. Artificial Intelligence – in house blue print and development.
5. Products – digital products in wearables, physical and tangible merchandise, trigger products.
6. Integration of A.I for medical treatment. – in house (3 years down the line)

P. What are the manufacturing and distribution plans?

We are into creating knowledge content and delivery – online in digital format and offline in print format. For offline we already have publications, publishers and printers.

Distribution channel is to utilize digital infrastructure and social media. We have the following domains under us –

www.mindhacknfsi.com
www.thehumanexcellencenetwork.com
www.getfitwithnik.co.in
and their respective Facebook and Instagram handles.

Q. What are the various risks involved in building the organization?

The various risks involved are as follows –

  i. Hiring and retaining the right kind of employees.

  ii. Initial cash flows and building up clientele.

iii. Time factor and perseverance (need team and staff to be vision centric and proactive)

 iv. Back end support to every department.

  v. Market penetration and awareness.

 vi. Fund Allocation and financial management.

R. In what way will the team de-risk those?

  i. Right kind of employees – the way there is a buyer persona, we will have the employee persona who aligns with our thought process, vision and aspirations with some technical expertise beneficial or complementary to existing team and is highly educated and open to new ideas and change. – Recruitment Process Head

 ii. Initial Cash flows and clientele – Cash flow to be controlled at all times, not to spend unnecessarily on marketing. Appointing a financial management consultant and aligning expenses with goals to be achieved and set for quarterly targets. Budget allocation. – Head of Business and Communication

iii. Time factor – set defined goals for the vision, departments and individual team member to be achieved in a specified time frame. – Strategist

 iv. Back end support – Developing and defining the connectivity and complimentary structure of every department and individual. – Head of Business and Communication

v. Market penetration and awareness – connecting with people and organizations and putting out the message as to who we are what we do and what we aim to achieve. – Head of Business and Communication

vi. Fund Allocation and financial management – budgets. – President of the Company/Chairman of the Board.

Monday, 24th October 2022
NIKHIL MADUSKAR
Co-Founder, The Human Excellence Network/ THENTECH LIFESTYLE

A I

CHAPTER SEVEN

Decipher google sheets

Sr. NoPurposeServicesPriceToolsRequirements

1Current and Development solutions for the facilityCentre AnalysisinclusiveFormsIntroduction letter

2Locality and demographicsMarket Analysis - RegionalinclusiveParametersList of Services

3Market placementCompetition AnalysisinclusiveData SheetBenefits

4Current and Development solutions for the facilityService AnalysisinclusiveParametersExecution process

5To understand the growth of the businessFinancial and Sales Structure/ProjectionsinclusiveStructureDeliverables

6Monthly marketing strategyMarketing ServicesseparateList of ServicesMemento

7Business presence and imageBrandingseparateParameters

8Technical knowledge and business managementStaff TrainingseparateStructure

9Business establishmentGym and Facility Set UpseparateStructure

S.O.P 1

STANDARD OPERATING PROCEDURE

FOR CORE TEAM MEMBERS

DIRECTOR OF BUSINESS DEVELOPMENT AND COMMUNICATION

The head of business development who makes sure that THEN generates revenue.

Designation held by - V

Sr. No.RoleResponsibiltiesGoalResources

1Products DevelopmentProduct and service ideationidea bankthink tank

Content Creationpublishingthink tank

Packagingexperiencevendors

Costs and Time Durationbudgetingfinance dept

Pricing and Placementrevenuethink tank

Deliveriesrevenuevendors

PerformancerevenueC.O.O

Phasing Out the Productstrategythink tank

2Systems and ReportsReporting Formats and Templatesintercom

E-mails and other communicationsextercom

Data Creation and Storageinternal data

Data Creation and Storageknowledge bank

3Voice of THENStaff external communicationvision dnaCo-founders

Customer Relationshipvision dnathink tank

Advertising and Marketing Languagevision dnamanuscript

Appearancemarket cred

4Collaborations and Tie UpsIdentify - Highlight - Study - Approachbrand/revenue

Approach Method Systemexperience

Contractuallegal bindingCOO

Pricing and Revenue GenerationrevenueCOO/Finance

Goodwill PartnersbrandingCOO

Performance of Collab/ tie ups reviewrevenueCOO

Broadcastingvision dnamanuscript

Awareness Programs Partnershipvision dnamanuscript

5Sales and Sales TargetMonthly & Quarterly Sale Target PlanrevenueSale Team 1

Department TargetsrevenueSale Team 1

Target for Self (Dept + your own)revenueSale Team 1

Collab Revenue TargetsrevenueSale Team 1

Joyson TargetsrevenueSale Team 1

Raj Individual TargetrevenueSale Team 1

Brand TargetsrevenueSale Team 1

6Taking it GlobalIdentify - Highlight - Study - Approachrevenue

Marketrevenue

Productrevenue

Servicerevenue

Brandsrevenue

Vision DNAexperience

ASSISTANT BUSINESS DEVELOPMENT EXECUTIVE

Assisting The DIrector of Business Development and Communications who makes sure that THEN generates revenue.

Designation held by - R

Sr. No.RoleResponsibiltiesGoalResources

1Assisting Business HeadAll activities and responsibilitiesTo

to be carried out as a delegateeaseHire

of VeenitaVeenita'sInterns

andworkloadStaff

Fill in gaps or remove roadblocksand increaseand

in Veenita's workefficiency andFire

Data Creation and Storageresults ofwith approvals

Data creation of your viewsthe company

2Company SecretaryInternal Meetings RecordoperationsCOO

Meetings ReviewoperationsCOO

Accounts and ExpenseoperationsCOO

Data maintenanceoperationsCOO

Records MaintenanceoperationsCOO

Staff/intern recordoperationsCOO

Legal documents maintenanceoperationsCOO

3Data AnalysisMarket Research for THEN productsRevenueVin and Joy

Background check of CollabsBrandingManuscript

Performance ReportsRevenueVin and Nik

Trigger SystemsOperationsCOO

Product DevelopmentRevenueCo-founders

4Admin HeadDaily work reportsoperationsVin

Staff SOP implementationoperationsCOO

Sales team reportsoperationsVin

Day to day accounts and expensesoperationsCOO

5Event Co-ordinatorSchedulingRevenueVin

Staffing

On site delivery

Requirement list

Execution

6Sales and Sales TargetTo assist business headRevenueVin

Individual TargetRevenue

ExecutionRevenue

Show me the moneyRevenue

6Business DevelopmentTo create

additional

avenues

for

revenue

generation
and achieve
company
revenue
targets
without
hampering
the functioning
of the system
CHIEF TRAINING OFFICER
Head of Training Services and Products which generate Revenue for THEN
Designation held by - J
Sr. No.RoleResponsibiltiesGoalResources
1Products DevelopmentProduct and service ideationidea bankthink tank
Packagingexperiencevendors
Deliveriesrevenuevendors
PerformancerevenueC.O.O
Training Contentrevenue
2Systems and ReportsTraining Reports Format & Tempinternal system
Training Reports Format & Tempexperience
Trainer Selection Systemoperations
Trainer Allotment Systemrevenue
Trainer Performance Reportexperience
Trainer Growth Systemrevenue
Product Development Systemidea bankthink tank
3Voice of THENStaff external communicationvision dnaCo-founders
(for trainers and serviceCustomer Relationshipvision dnathink tank

providers of THEN)Advertising and Marketing Languagevision dnamanuscript

Appearancemarket cred

4Collaborations and Tie UpsIdentify - Highlight - Study - Approachbrand/revenue

Individualsinvest/rev

Professionalsrevenue

Artists and Creatorsbrand/revenue

Addictive Products and Producersbrand/revenue

Citiesinvest/revVin

5Sales and Sales TargetOnline Sale Targetrevenue

Offline Sale Targetrevenue

Product Salerevenue

Individual Staff Targetsrevenue

Self Targetsrevenue

Collab Targetsrevenue

Fitness and Sports Club Consultancy

Sr. NoPurposeServicesPriceToolsRequirements

1Current and Development solutions for the facilityCentre AnalysisinclusiveFormsIntroduction letter

2Locality and demographicsMarket Analysis - RegionalinclusiveParametersList of Services

3Market placementCompetition AnalysisinclusiveData SheetBenefits

4Current and Development solutions for the facilityService AnalysisinclusiveParametersExecution process

5To understand the growth of the businessFinancial and Sales Structure/ProjectionsinclusiveStructureDeliverables

6Monthly marketing strategyMarketing ServicesseparateList of ServicesMemento

7Business presence and imageBrandingseparateParameters

8Technical knowledge and business managementStaff TrainingseparateStructure

9Business establishmentGym and Facility Set UpseparateStructure

How to explain the services?

Greetings,

I hope I have not called you in the busy moment, as I have an investment proposition for you in terms of health and well- being.

"Target response"

No, I am definitely not selling you any insurance policy here, but I am calling from The Human Excellence Network just to know if you are doing fine in terms of health and mental well-being and if you are happy in the general sense of terms.

" "

We at The Human Excellence Network are here to listen and I am making this call to help you in the best possible of ways.

" "

The whole idea of finding answers or of making life better is through the way of MINDFULNESS. The word mindfulness means to become aware.

" "

The Human Excellence Network has the primary code called THE MINDFUL PROGRAM and the approach is H.U.M.A.N

H – Health

U – Understanding

M – Movement

A – Awareness and

N – Nourishment

" "

If you would like to know more

Yes – continue

NO – How about I call you some other time suitable for you and in the meantime forward you the details on mail or on your WhatsApp number? (even if no still send the details)

Yes – continue

What makes us truly happy? Our friends, our family, our fun time. How about "we make our own happiness" being happy and feeling good from the inside. What do you think?"

" "

Life has its ups and downs and if someone is saying Life is all good is just trying to sell you something and investing is the new price, but it brings in good results and that is what we do here at The Human Excellence Network.

" "

Well, we have various programs and courses that will not only benefit you in terms of health and well-being but shall also help you in your career and personal life goals.

" "

The various programs we have, fall under 3 basic categories and we have tie-ups with multiple brands which are here to cater for you and those categories are

a. Education and Knowledge

b. Training and Exercise

c. Food and Nourishment

What would be your choice?

" "

Education and Knowledge involves courses on Exercise Science and Food Science which will not only help you understand yourself better as to your relationship with food and movement but also help you in building a career in the fitness industry.

Training and Exercise is powered by _ and The_ which are online as well as offline exercise programs be it for losing weight or getting fitter.

_ is about making exercise fun and intense while THE DEN is all about hard-core technique oriented physical training.

We make sure that you stay motivated and focused by our approach in the training and you having fun while exploring your strengths and overcoming your weaknesses. It is all about going for the new high.

Food and nourishment is under the guidance of "GET FIT WITH NIK" which has a personalised approach to food habits and diet which are customised to your needs and goals and also addressing any health issues that you may be facing and our tagline is "Nurture and Rejuvenate with Food."

We all love to eat food and in GET FIT WITH NIK we help you build your relationship with food. It is ALL ABOUT FOOD AND YOU. If you happen to be staying in Pune, we also have meals provided by our food partner "_" which provides healthy meals at your doorstep.

How would you like to proceed and which service would be your preference?

" "

Actions - Send the Forms to fill up

Our forms are designed so that you spend some time with your own self and answer the questions which are close to your mind, body, heart and soul. Your answers are safe with us and we maintain a fiduciary relationship with our clients because we believe in personal relations and the importance of one's privacy, like a doctor patient relationship. We THE HUMAN EXCELLENCE NETWORK

ARE HERE TO LISTEN and we shall do the follow ups necessary for your needs. It is a network for you.

Good day and take care.

SEE YOU THEN.

CHAPTER EIGHT

MindHack

MINDHACK
DIGITAL STRUCTURE FOR GYM APP

A. Welcome digital kit

- Personal address
- Introduction to the gym and the services.
- What is achieved by using the app and how it gives continuous benefits.

A. Customer bio-data input/details/data storage

- Age, gender, height, weight, occupation, hometown, education and other personal info.
- Biometrics or Body analysis report – bmi, body fat percentage, muscle mass, etc.
- Medical conditions
- Fitness Goals
- Food habits and preferences.
- Attendance and reason for absence or skipping workout.
- Gym membership and other services

C. Customer Engagement

- Workout diary
- Food diary
- Basic Workout Schedules
- Paid Workout Schedules
- Basic Diet Plans
- Member Achievements/celebrity of the month
- Access to blogs, articles, fb pages and Instagram
- Member Connect (optional)
- Shopping Cart – Merchandise and other products and services.

D. MOST IMPORTANT – THE PURPOSE

- Only one user and one device per app.
- Once bio data is filled in, it should lock in the app and no changes can be made.
- Data mining and data base.
- Revenue Generation – present continuous.
- Member engagement and member retention.
- To be available on android and IOS.
- No annoying notifications – once every Sunday at a specific hour.
- To make my life and business easier to manage so that I can focus on research and study.

E. My Questions and pointers for the App Developer –

1. Feasibility? Cost? Expense breakdown?

(Yash had pointed out that clients try to do everything at once which makes it an expensive affair and it is better to go step by step)

2. Digital infrastructure – storage, backend support, tweaks and improvements? (Got a brief idea from the both of you. Need detailed info so that I can put it down on paper)

3. The company that I worked for before had hired an app developer company and the app was being developed and deployed in phases (pre-Covid 2017-20, all came to a stop in lockdown because of failure to pay dues and data was inaccessible because of mismanagement on part of my company).

The overall cost of the same was high if ROI is considered as it was more of a gym management app and did not generate any revenue by itself. The app should be able to generate revenue by itself and at least pay for itself.

4. Can the app be made – to be used by gyms where I can licence it out to them and primarily for individual customers.

5. The gym app will be a small project compared to what I envision for the nutrition. Understanding the process is important for me.

6. Such apps do exist which are available for use on subscription basis which range from 300rs per month to annual usage fee of 70k. Why to have your own app and is it feasible to have your own app developed?

CHAPTER NINE

website

THE HUMAN EXCELLENCE NETWORK

DRIVING EXCELLENCE IN HUMAN PROGRESS

COLLABORATING EXCELLENCE IN THE FIELD OF FITNESS SCIENCE AND HEALTHCARE

T.H.E.N - THE HUMAN EXCELLENCE NETWORK

Open Ended Platform

During the COVID-19 pandemic, the battle between a virus and our survival, the necessity of building a strong immune system in every individual is the first and foremost line of defense against any diseases was realized.

While scientists and doctors were finding a cure, people realized the need of exercise and good nutrition habits to lead a healthy life.

With the world under a lockdown, we realized the need of a virtual existence and online work from home market activities, which led to growth of IT and software companies changing the way we do business and developments in artificial intelligence and machine learning.

This period of dread brought in a paradigm shift in universal consciousness and has led to a path of collaboration for human excellence instead of competing for just numbers and figures. A lot of technology is becoming an open ended platform for sharing of knowledge and developments.

On the same lines, T.H.E.N - The Human Excellence Network is an open ended platform for collaborating excellence in the field of fitness science, nutrition, health, medical care, mental well-being, human performance and spirituality to drive human progress.

T.H.E.N also includes the IT and Software industry on this platform as AI and machine learning is the present continuous future in human health and performance.

Our Approach

Our approach is based in the roots of self reflection and self realization through which an individual and mankind can unlock the potential towards excellence. And in taking the vision forward, T.H.E.N is taking the steps of -

- Knowledge creation and education
- Training Programs
- Research and Development
- Awareness and Social Welfare
- Collaborations and Tie ups
- Healthcare
- Intuitive A.I

The vision having a wider expanse makes it a collaborative effort and the notion of one world a necessary reality to drive human progress.

WELCOME TO THE NETWORK

There's much to see here. So, take your time, look around, and learn all there is to know about us. T.H.E.N being an open ended platform invites you not just to bring in positive change in your ownself but to also make an impact in human progress

ABOUT US

Start with the Why

We are expert professionals with a vast experience in the fitness industry who are driven by passion and a vision to help the society inculcate the life skills of exercise and nutrition in order to help individuals achieve higher potential and lead a better holistic lifestyle.

The Human Movement

Every new century of man's timeline brings in a wave of pandemics and other catastrophes both man-made and natural which shake the foundations of the society and leads to a new era of human excellence and with the same virtue of perseverance, we at T.H.E.N aim to drive excellence in human progress. It is the "I" in each of us that strives for better life for oneself, loved ones and for mankind as a whole.

Universal Consciousness

The human brain is said to be on the similar lines of the universe. The universe is said to be conscious and can be shown through experiments on the tiniest part of energy particles. We are made from the elements that are abundant in the universe and as per spirituality the universe is within you. Like the one who meditates while energy enlightens the consciousness within the one who meditates, so are we connected to the universe and the time has come for human excellence as man progresses and makes advances in technology. The future is now - a present continuous towards excellence. And it starts with "I"

SERVICES

EDUCATION AND AWARENESS - Education and Training in the field of fitness science. With courses such as Foundations of Fitness, Certified Personal Trainer, Sports Nutrition, Nutrition, Women Health, Biomechanics and Human Performance , Sports Psychology and various other educational courses in training methods and approach.

ONLINE AND OFFLINE TRAINING PROGRAMS - Custom made training programs inculcating the values of The Mindful Project in improving human performance from a recreational athlete to professional sportsmen and from corporate wellness to all age groups irrespective of work profession.

CORPORATE WELLNESS - To achieved the work life balance, one needs to spend time with one's ownself and needs to exercise and have balanced meals. Exercise activates the mind muscle connection while nutrition fuels the body and mind. We customize programs as per your needs and work schedule and inculcate a better approach towards a better you be it a fresher to the hardworking CEO or the firm decision maker Chairman. We all work and make an impact so let us guide you to a better lifestyle with exercise and food.

HEALTH AND HYGIENE PRODUCTS - We are aware of the need of health and hygeine products as part of lifestyle and in pursuit of that we collaborate for selling, distribution and developments of such products which are thoughtful and effective in dealing with human well-being.

COLLABORATING EXCELLENCE - T.H.E.N is an open ended platform and in being true to it's roots is open for collaboration with medical professionals and other brands and business making an impact in the field of fitness, nutrition, health, healthcare and otther activities which help in making a qualitative change in human life and society at at large. We look forward to putting your brand forward.

DATA ANALYSIS, DATA COLLECTION AND MARKET RESEARCH - Development is based on data and the deployment of the same to create solutions. We provide data analysis and data collection with Market Research for Fitness and Health Industry with our very owm team of researchers and analysts.

RESEARCH AND DEVELOPMENT - With MindHack NFSI as our department of knowledge creation and content, we are equipped with resources dealing in research and development work in the field of fitness, human performance, nutrition, healthcare, mental health, neuroscience, spirituality and AI.

ACADEMY - Offline education and training programs to inculcate the knowledge of fitness and health. From the gym to the classroom and from the field to the workbook. An organized practical approach towards training and knowledge.

AWARENESS AND SOCIAL WELFARE PROGRAMS - Conducting awareness and wellness programs across all stratas of the society. No Individual Left Behind. The philosophy being that individuals make up the society and that society is for welfare of the individual. Inspired by Bentham's Theory of Law, we work for the upliftment of every individual by spreading awareness and sharing of knowledge while creating an eco-system for self reflection and self realization.

CHAPTER TEN

MEMORANDUM OF UNDERSTANDING

THIS MEMORANDUM OF UNDERSTANDING IS BEING EXECUTED ON THIS 31ST DAY OF AUGUST 2022 BETWEEN DRAFTED BY NIKHIL MADUSKAR. THE UNDERSTANDING BETWEEN THE THREE PARTIES IS AS FOLLOWS -

WHEREAS,

ALL THE ABOVE THREE PARTIES TO THIS MOU ARE WORKING AS CERTIFIED /QUALIFIED/ EXPERIENCED FITNESS AND HEALTH CONSULTANTS/TRAINERS IN THE FITNESS INDUSTRY AND THEY HAVE MUTUALLY AGREED TO COME TOGETHER TO ESTABLISH/FORM A NEW COMPANY/LEGAL ENTITY BY THE NAME OF "THE HUMAN EXCELLENCE NETWORK."

THE DETAILS OF THIS MOU ARE AS FOLLOWS –

1. ALL THE ABOVE THREE PARTIES SHALL BE CONSIDERED TO BE AS THE CO-FOUNDERS OF THE HUMAN EXCELLENCE NETWORK. THE ADDITION OF A PROMOTER AS WELL AS OF ANOTHER PERSON WILL DEEMED TO BE CONSIDERED AS CO-FOUNDER ON RECOMMENDATION OF PARTY

THREE. THE EXISTING NUMBER OF CO-FOUNDERS ON THIS DAY IS THREE AND SHALL NOT EXCEED FIVE IN THE LIFETIME OF THE HUMAN EXCELLENCE NETWORK.

2. ALL THE THREE PARTIES TO THIS MOU HAVE MUTUALLY AGREED TO TAKE FORWARD THE VISION OF THE HUMAN EXCELLENCE NETWORK AS LAID OUT IN THE BUSINESS PLAN ATTACHED WITH THIS MOU AND HAVE ALSO AGREED TO WORK TO PROMOTE THE VISION AND MISSION WITH UTMOST HONESTY AND SINCERITY OF THEIR HEART AND CHARACTER.

3. THIS MOU SHALL BE THE BASIS OF ESTABLISHMENT OF AND FORMATION OF A COMPANY NAMED THE HUMAN EXCELLENCE NETWORK ALSO TO BE KNOWN AS T.H.E.N.

4. THE POINTS OF CONTRACT SHARED ON MAIL BETWEEN THE THREE PARTIES PRIOR TO THE EXECUTION OF THIS MOU ARE BINDING ON ALL THE THREE PARTIES AND THEY ARE AS FOLLOWS –

POINTS OF CONTRACT

A. STAKE/EQUITY – Each Co-Founder to receive minimum 5% to maximum 10% of equity without investment but as a sense of ownership towards T.H.E.N. This equity will be subject to certain conditions such as non-transferability and any other condition deemed beneficial for the progress of T.H.E.N.

Additional Stakes can be purchased by the Co-Founders by investing the money as per valuation deemed fit by the Board and the Core Team as a whole.

B. REMUNERATION –

i. A basic remuneration of Rs. 15,000/- to be paid to every Co-Founder on monthly basis which may be adjusted or paid out as per the availability of funds and financial efficacy of THEN.

ii. Every Co-Founder shall be paid an additional amount out of the revenue after deduction of expenses. Such an amount shall be percentage of the revenue less expense and the said amount so derived will be divided amongst the Co-founders equally.

iii. To compute the annual take home salaries of the Co-Founders, man hours will be kept as record when conducting a special class or activity of utmost importance and non-availability of the others.

iv. All the above remunerations to be paid only after taking into consideration the functioning and efficacy of THEN and no such payment shall lead to withholding or functioning of THEN.

C. PERSONAL BRANDS AND TIE- UPS –

The Human Excellence Network being an open ended platform for collaborating excellence in the progress of mankind, wishes and wills to preserve the identity of every individual associated with it be it directly and indirectly as well as maintain the individual identity of brands associated with.

i. The existing brands, businesses, intellectual property or any idea envisioned by the Co-Founders before the formation of THEN shall remain the exclusive ownership of the respective Co-Founders and THEN shall have no claim nor interest in the same.

ii. The Co-Founders can use THEN platform to promote and conduct their individual brand business at a price or cost not less than 10% of the revenue derived from the platform. The upper limit shall be fixed only after mutual agreement of all Co-Founders and stake holders.

iii. Any new brands or concepts derived by the Co-Founders after the establishment of the platform, shall be considered as part of THEN. This is in order to promote the vision of The Human Excellence Network. The Blue Print of the Network gives the indication of expansion and the umbrella of activities that fall under the network.

iv. Books and any other publications including digital will be the sole ownership of those who create it and THEN shall have the right to use the said material with mentioning the credits at all time.

v. At all times, the platform shall recognize and highlight the contributing artists wherever it can. Artists are all those who play an important role in the activities of the platform right from the man who gets us tea to the greatest contributor of all. Every act is worth a mention.

D. Initial Arrangement and Structuration –

To commence the work of THEN, we shall be using the Proprietorship MindHack NFSI for entering into contracts and agreements with third parties and using Bank account of the same. MindHack NFSI is the proprietorship of Nikhil

Maduskar and is currently inactive.

All Agreements and contracts entered by MindHack NFSI from this day onward that is the signing of this MOU shall be deemed to be that of THE HUMAN EXCELLENCE NETWORK. All payments received from this date onwards shall be considered to be belonging to THEN.

This arrangement is valid only till a proper legal entity of THEN has been created.

All documents and identifications will consist of both names – THE HUMAN EXCELLENCE NETWORK and MindHack NFSI till entity of THEN is established.

E.   FUNDING AND EQUITY DISTRIBUTION

Under this MOU, All the Co-Founders shall be considered as to owning equal percentage of stake in THEN.

All Co-Founders are aware that there will be a need of raising funds as well as get a partner on board who can invest and fund the Network and the same need not be an active partner or stake holder.

All Co-Founders are aware of the goal of creating the Network into a corporate of multiples of wealth and a long standing one, and hence the need to structure the entity in such a way to promote the growth of the Network on a wider socio-economic front.

All Co-Founders are aware that they shall have to let go a part of their stake in order to allow inflow of capital and investment. At no times will the stake of each Co-Founder go below 5% for the next 3 years till the Network reaches for an IPO.

The stake of the Founders and Promoters shall at no time fall below 20% of the total equity for the next 5 years in order to maintain the integrity of the vision.

A Financial Expert will be hired to form the structuration of THEN and a road map for growth shall also be drafted.

F. Active Participation as per their roles and responsibilities are expected from the Founders and a quarterly peer review shall be done by the Core Team to further lead the vision and keep an active effort to promote the same.

5. ALL THE ACTIVITIES WILL BEAR THE NAME "THE HUMAN EXCELENCE NETWORK" (T.H.E.N.) AND THE PROMOTIONS AND MARKETING AND ANY SORT OF COMMUNICATION MADE SHALL BE DONE UNDER THE SAID NAME.

6. THE NAME OF MINDHACK NFSI SHALL BE USED ALONG WITH THE HUMAN EXCELLENCE NETWORK AS AND WHEN REQUIRED FOR THE LEGALITY OF THE OPERATIONS TILL THE HUMAN EXCELLENCE NETWORK IS REGISTERED AS A LEGAL ENTITY AS DEEMED FIT. WITHIN FORTY-FIVE DAYS (45 DAYS) FROM THE EXECUTION OF THIS MOU, THE HUMAN EXCELLENCE NETWORK LEGAL ENTITY SHALL BE ESTABLISHED I.E. BY 15TH OF OCTOBER 2022.

7. OTHER THAN BEING THE CO-FOUNDER WILL BE ASSIGNED THE FOLLOWING ROLES AND DESIGNATION AT THE HUMAN EXCELLENCE NETWORK-

THE ROLES AND RESPONISIBILTIES SHALL BE AS DEPICTED IN THE DIAGRAM IN THE BUSINESS PLAN.

THE SOPS AND OTHER DOCUMENTS FOR INTERNAL OPERATIONS SHALL BE DRAFTED WITH THE GUIDANCE OF EXPERT PROFESSIONALS TO HAVE A CLEAR DETAILED STRUCTURE OF ROLES AND RESPONSIBILTIES.

8. IF ANY DISPUTE ARISES BETWEEN THE PARTIES, THEN THE SAME SHALL BE SETTLED AMICABLY BY NEGOTIATIONS BETWEEN THE TWO PARTIES. IF SUCH NEGOTIATIONS FAIL THEN TWO PARTIES CAN RESOLVE THE MATTER BY ARBITRATION IN ACCORDANCE WITH THE INDIAN ARBITRATION ACT.

9. PLACE OF JURISDICTION – PUNE.

10. CONFIDENTIALITY – ALL THE PARTIES TO THIS MOU SHALL MAINTAIN THE CONFIDENTIALITY OF THE DATA CREATED AND GENERATED IN THE ACTIVITIES OF THE HUMAN EXCELLENCE NETWORK AND SHALL UPHOLD THE VISION OF THE HUMAN EXCELLENCE NETWORK AT ALL COST AND AT ALL TIMES. ALL RIGHTS AND PRIVILEGES BELONG WITH THE HUMAN EXCELLENCE NETWORK IN PURSUIT OF THE VISION SET IN WHILE GIVING DUE CREDIT TO THOSE WHO DESERVE AND PARTICIPATE.

11. ON THIS DAY OF EXECUTION OF THIS MOU OF THE HUMAN EXCELLENCE NETWORK, ALL THE THREE PARTIES SHALL BE CONSIDERED AS EQUAL AND HAVE EQUAL DISTRIBUTION OF THE STAKE IN T.H.E.N. AND HAVE MUTUALLY AGREED TO

DIVEST/LET GO/ ADJUST EQUALLY AS PER THE STAKE/EQUITY CLAUSE FROM THE POINTS OF CONTRACT MENTIONED ABOVE.

12. ALL PARTIES SHALL CO-OPERATE AT ALL TIMES TO TAKE THE VISION FORWARD AND MAKE THE VISION A REALITY.

THIS MOU SHALL COME INTO FORCE ON THIS DAY OF 31ST OF AUGUST 2022 ON SIGNING OF AND EXECUTION BY ALL THREE PARTIES.
THE HUMAN EXCELLENCE NETWORK BEGINS!
DATE – 31ST AUGUST 2022
PLACE – PUNE